Construction Realtors

Transforming Real Estate.

The Pocket Guide Introduction

Founders

Luis Moro and Morgan Mainz

Written By

Luis Moro

RECONA: Real Estate Construction Agency

Construction Realtors

Transforming Real Estate.

The Pocket Guide Introduction

Published by
Transparent Technologies, Inc

Construction Realtors

Transforming Real Estate

Mission

Create Real Estate Value for Everyone

Vision

Everyone Loves Their Home

Principles

1) Produce Real Estate Value People can
- *a. See*
- *b. Measure*
- *c. Experience*
- *d. With Integrity*

2) Always Learning New Principles

DEDICATION

For our families, friends, and
associates who empower us.

To the Real Estate Professionals
who make the American Dream come true.

With the people who allow us to empower them.

CONTENTS

x

ACKNOWLEDGMENT

To all our friends and family; including associates, colleagues, and people we've met that have given us, Morgan Mainz and Luis Moro, the education, training, abilities, and character to take on transforming the consumer construction market.

We have started a journey, that will grow with many, and continue into the future well beyond us with future leaders.

We would like to acknowledge in advance the Construction Realtors and the Real Estate Professionals that are committed to creating a new realm of consumer construction integrity.

As we expand, Construction Realtors will lead the way and continuing make a difference with everyone committed to having their American Dream come true.

RECONA: Real Estate Construction Agency

"When you know how to actually build Real Estate.

You know the real value of Real Estate"

Construction Realtors

RECONA: Real Estate Construction Agency

INTRODUCTION

This Construction Realtor pocket guide servers as "context creator" for the future of real estate sales, buying, and developing.

Being a Construction Realtor is a natural evolution for creating the most value for people when we engage in the Real Estate market.

The Construction Realtors in any real estate office have the knowledge-base home owners can use to create the most value for their homes. This new generation of Construction Realtors know how to provide information and resources that actually create measurable value for Real Estate.

Construction Realtors provide value clients can see, measure, and experience for the life of the real estate.

While people should expect the customary market analysis, community reports, and fancy marketing materials from Realtors and Real Estate Agents.

Construction Realtors are the exception who know what it actually takes to create real value for Real Estate. Construction Realtors have the trusted qualified resources to deliver results.

"The Construction Realtors in any real estate office have the knowledge base, home owners can use to create the most value for their homes."

RECONA: Real Estate Construction Agency

1 CONSTRUCTION REALTORS

- Construction Realtors are the A-Lister's of Real Estate Sales, Buying, and Developing.

- Construction Realtors create quantifiable value for clients Real Estate investment.

- Construction Realtors continuously educate, train, and develop themselves in one of the most important elements of the real estate business. Increasing the value of Real Estate.

- Construction Realtors work in residential, commercial, corporate, and government real estate offices.

"Construction Realtors
provide value clients can

see,

measure, and

experience."

2 THE ART OF CREATING REAL ESTATE VALUE

The most successful real estate investments and ventures are the properties that *can be* maximized to their fullest financial gain in any market.

The key here is Real Estate that *"can be"* maximized.

- Construction Realtors know how to distinguish potential Real Estate value.

- Construction Realtors know how to create new measurable value for Real Estate.

- Construction Realtors have and deliver the teams to maximize Real Estate value.

- Whether you are buying or selling, or developing Real Estate, Construction Realtors are the clients competitive advantage.

"Construction Realtors can see the potential construction value of real estate before others do."

3 THE POWER OF CONSTRUCTION REALTORS

Sooner or later, all Real Estate needs construction solutions. Along with being professional Real Estate Agents;

- Construction Realtors are educated in construction solutions.

- Construction Realtors have a keen mindset for creative construction solutions.

- Construction Realtors know the trusted professionals in their community.

- Construction Realtors empower construction professionals to deliver with integrity.

- The Construction Realtors network has a deep wealth of creative, resourceful, construction knowledge and how-to in the seven major construction solutions.

RECONA: Real Estate Construction Agency

4 THE SEVEN MAJOR CONSUMER CONSTRUCTION SOLUTIONS

1. Custom Building: Unique homes for unique lifestyles.

2. Upgrades: Interior improvements maximizing resources.

3. Remodeling: Interior transformation producing new value.

4. Renovation: Exterior perfections improving the community.

5. Landscape: Exterior beatification distinguishing homes.

6. Additions: Smart sustainable development.

7. Consulting: The Competitive Advantage. Always be learning and training.

Knowledge and relationships are the foundation of Construction Realtors.

RECONA: Real Estate Construction Agency

5 CONSTRUCTION REALTOR PRINCIPLES

Construction Realtors work with professionals who know the importance of honoring and following construction principles, while simultaneously adapting to each unique project condition to deliver the greatest value for each client.

- With today's Internet, everyone has access to construction information.
- With today's options, everyone has potential with diverse solutions.

Through all this information access, construction principles must be known and managed to produce the best possible results.

- To be successful in Construction, it's best to know as many of the terms (jargon) used in the construction industry.
- It best to know the positions and job responsibilities of the people providing the solutions.

Construction Realtors can guide clients through the many moving parts of construction.

With emerging construction solutions, the future of real estate will continue to transform. Additional volumes of Construction Realtors will provide examples, case studies, and explore options for the seven major consumer construction solutions.

"Construction Realtors work with professionals who know the importance of honoring their word."

6 CONSTRUCTION REALTOR MASTERY

Masterful Construction Realtors study the art of skilled craftsmanship that produces real estate value for generations to come.

Mastery in construction requires knowing the tools of the trade. Including:

- Hardware to the best construction equipment.

- Appropriate materials and appliances.

- How to masterfully unite these creative tools building undeniable construction quality as an art form.

All of these factors need to be wrapped up and presented with the most effective interior and exterior design.

At any stage of creating real estate value, the most advanced real estate agents are Construction Realtors.

They know the process, they understand the foundation of real estate value from the idea to ground breaking and up to the perfect custom-built home.

Construction Realtors know the tools of the Art.

"Make no mistake about it.

Construction is a creative collaborate Art.

Construction Realtors are creative collaborative Artist."

RECONA: Real Estate Construction Agency

7 CONSTRUCTION REALTORS KNOW REAL ESTATE

Construction Realtors continuously educate, train, and develop their Real Estate value creating Art.

- Construction Realtors create the opportunities for legitimate real estate value growth.

- Construction Realtors understand the Real Estate value growth process from idea through long-term real estate value growth.

- Construction Realtors help guide the physically improvement of value in Real Estate for clients.

- Construction Realtors create value clients can actually see, measure, and experience.

- Construction Realtors are a reliable resource for consumer construction solutions.

- Construction Realtors know Real Estate.

RECONA: Real Estate Construction Agency

8 HOW TO BECOME A CONSTRUCTION REALTOR

Like anything worth taking on in life. To become a Construction Realtor requires a declaration. Simply declare you're committed to becoming a Construction Realtor.

"I AM a Construction Realtor"

Keep saying "I AM a Construction Realtor" until you experience it.

Simultaneously start learning the construction distinctions you need to know to master construction.

Your real estate agents sales skills, combined with your real estate construction skills will start to give you the ultimate competitive advantage. No gimmicks. You can actually create and produce real value for your real estate clients.

You can help, guide, consult, and even project manage real estate construction solutions for your clients.

There is no mystery to being the best.

- The best know how to create solutions for problems.

- The best know professionals who know solutions for problems.

- The best create value for people.

Construction Realtors create real value for people.

Every day, declare you're a Construction Realtor and stay on the path of mastering construction solutions that add value for each of your real estate clients.

"Construction Realtors and their RECONA network deliver visible value for clients."

RECONA: Real Estate Construction Agency

9 CONSTRUCTION REALTORS TRANSFORMING REAL ESTATE

Construction Realtors was created by Luis Moro and Morgan Mainz to empower real estate agents committed to delivering real, measureable, real estate value for their real estate clients.

Luis and Morgan united their experience, knowledge-base, and know how, with their relationships and unstopped commitment to transform consumer construction experiences.

Luis and Morgan created this unique consumer construction business process to transform consumer construction solutions, while empowering the professionals who deliver the solutions with integrity.

Construction Realtors is Powered by RECONA, the Real Estate Construction Agency; a home base where local qualified construction professionals can obtain opportunities to provide consumer construction solutions with integrity, fair margins, and the partnership of Construction Realtors.

Construction Realtors are leading the way to transform consumer construction.

With the construction solutions available today, there is no reason for a client or construction professional to be taken advantage.

The consumer construction market wants a new level of performance, integrity, and accountability.

- The clients want it.

- The credible builders want it.

- The honest contractors, skilled professionals, and labor also want new levels of integrity.

There are plenty of honest, qualified, construction professionals who love building, loving solving construction problems, and are not interested in lying, cheating, and stealing for a living.

Construction Realtors empower other construction associates through the process of delivering quality clients, who obtain quality solutions, from quality professionals.

ABOUT THE FOUNDERS
LUIS MORO AND MORGAN MAINZ

Both Morgan Mainz and Luis Moro are diverse veterans in the real estate business.

Combined, they have the range of experience and know how required to transform consumer construction.

They both know it will take a new generation of construction professionals uniting to do it.

Morgan Mainz is a third-generation builder in Santa Barbara, California. He grew up on construction sites with his father and uncle. The Mainz family where trail blazing custom homes, commercial properties, and other now high-end wealth real estate in California.

Morgan is a true Construction Artist. Morgan's mastery of custom home building expands from the most detailed craftsman's touch, to the latest technology solar home. Morgan is immersed in all the building solutions and diverse collaborations required to create and build true real estate value.

Morgan's built real estate around the world.

Luis Moro has thirty years of real estate and mortgage sales, training, and development. Coming from a construction family history in Cuba. He has twenty-five years' experience in "transformational business architecture." Luis has the skill set and mindset required to create and produce scalable sustainable business models required to transform the consumer construction market.

Luis created the Being "Trainable" methodology used in creating fully functioning, self-determining teams. "Trainable" emerged from his work with Professional Parents committed to raising fully functioning, self-determining children.

Luis has trained and developed people worldwide.

Construction Realtors

Construction Realtors is an opportunity for Real Estate Professionals to unite and transform The consumer construction market. Making the American Dream a worthy opportunity for everyone.

Learn more about Morgan Mainz and Luis Moro at ConstructionRealtors.com

Construction Realtors

Transforming Real Estate

Powered by RECONA

RECONA: Real Estate Construction Agency

AFTERWORD

Thank you for seeing if being a Construction Realtors is for you. Construction Realtors can be found in both residential, commercial, corporate, and government real estate offices. They are real estate professionals committed to Transforming Real Estate. United, we create and produce more value than individually.

In business, we are either creating or empowering sales. Construction Realtors produce sales. Being a Construction Realtor is designed for people who are the A-Listers of real estate delivering value to their clients and community.

We are powered by RECONA, The Real Estate Construction Agency.

RECONA is a network of construction professionals who empower the sales Construction Realtors create. RECONA professionals are the people who produce the construction solutions Construction Realtors offer.

We all need each other. The clients, the Construction Realtors, and the RECONA professionals. We all want to win. Becoming a Construction Realtor powered by RECONA ensures we all win together, with integrity.

For more information on how to be part of Construction Realtors and The Real Estate Construction Agency visit Recona.us

Together we're transforming real estate.

RECONA: Real Estate Construction Agency

www.ingramcontent.com/pod-product-compliance
Lightning Source LLC
Chambersburg PA
CBHW071244220526
45468CB00002B/994